21 Easy Ukulele Folk Songs

BEGINNING UKULELE SONGS BOOK 5

FOR SOPRANO, CONCERT AND TENOR
UKULELES
WITH C TUNING (G, C, E, A)

Rebecca Bogart and Jenny Peters

This book includes a free online video course.

To see a sample video visit

ukulele.io/FolkVideo

Book Layout ©2017 BookDesignTemplates.com

Ordering Information:
Quantity sales. Special discounts are available on quantity purchases by corporations, associations, and others. For details, contact the authors at the address above.

21 Easy Ukulele Folk Songs. —1st ed.
ISBN-13: 9781795608350

Do You Want to Play Folk and Blues Songs?

Learning folk music doesn't have to be frustrating with *21 Easy Ukulele Folk Songs*. We've put careful thought into creating great-sounding yet easy-to-play versions of favorite traditional songs. We've arranged the book so you can master the easiest music first and then gradually tackle harder tunes as your skills improve.

If you've learned the C, F, and G7 chords and a few basic strums, then this book is for you.

What Songs Are Included?

You'll find a nice mix of classic folk and blues songs with a bit of history about each song:

- Lovely Evening
- Lil' Liza Jane
- Happy Birthday
- Go Tell Aunt Rhody
- Wabash Cannonball
- Big Rock Candy Mountain
- Worried Man Blues
- St. Louis Blues
- Goodnight, Irene
- Down by the Riverside
- Sometimes I Feel Like a Motherless Child
- Sakura
- All through the Night
- Beautiful Dreamer
- Molly Malone
- Shenandoah
- The Ash Grove
- Take Me Out to the Ball Game
- Turkey in the Straw
- My Bonnie Lies Over the Ocean
- Sweet Betsy from Pike

Lots of Ways to Play Each Song

You can either sing the song and strum the chords or you can play the melody. All of the songs are written out on a standard music staff with a treble clef. Lyrics appear below the musical notation, and a chord letter appears above it each time there's a chord change. If you play by ear, the lyrics and chord changes are all you need. If you read music, you can learn the melody and rhythm from the standard music notation.

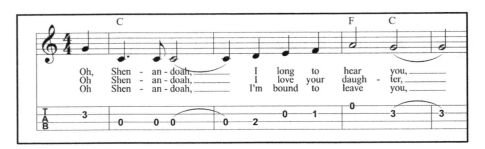

If you have a friend or family member who plays ukulele, you can create duets, with one person playing melody and the other one strumming chords. That's because below the music staff is a tab staff that works like a road map showing you how to pluck the melody on the strings of the ukulele.

We usually suggest several strumming patterns for each song. Some strums are easier when you are first learning a song, and some are more difficult so you can upgrade to a more complicated rhythm as you gain more skill.

Includes Free Online Video Course

Each song has an accompanying online lesson video with lyrics and chord changes so you can hear as well as see the music. It's a very fun and friendly way to learn musical skills. To set up your account at our website, please follow the directions in the section at the end of the book called "How to Access Your Free Video Course at ukulele.io."

Contents

About This Book

Welcome to *21 Easy Ukulele Folk Songs!* We're glad you're here. Before we get started: if you see a word in ***bold italics***, that means it's defined in a glossary we keep updated at ukulele.io/glossary. There's also a Chord Glossary with photos and chord stamps for the most common ukulele chords at the end of the book.

Don't Miss Out on Your Free Video Course!

Hey, we just wanted to remind you that you get a free video course with purchase of this book. The videos can help answer questions you might not even know you had. They also make learning ukulele easier and more fun. You'll see exactly how to place your hands to do the strums and make the chords. You'll be able to hear exactly how the chords and strums should sound. And if you don't know one of the songs or if you don't read music, the videos will help you hear how the songs go.

Each chapter of the book has its own matching unit in the video course. In the back of the book is a section with step by step instructions and screenshots to show you how to access your free course at our website, ukulele.io. Or you can visit ukulele.io/access-free-video-course.

In the free lesson videos included with your book, Jenny performs a simple arrangement of each tune, singing and strumming the melody first, then fingerpicking the melody on her ukulele. This approach lets you see two ways of playing the song. Use your own imagination and preferences to come up with a way that works best for you. If you have a friend to play with, you could:

1. Sing and strum one or two verses.
2. One person plays the melody and the other strums the chords.
3. Sing and strum another verse nd/or chorus to round out the song.

We've included some of the songs in several ***keys***. That's because some keys are easier for playing, and some keys are easier for singing. You could play a song first in one key, change keys using a ***bridge,*** and then continue in the second key. Our arrangement of "Sweet Betsy from Pike" does this in the keys of C and G major.

We've also included several versions of some of the songs, including some chord melody (solo ukulele) arrangements. Playing these arrangements will require more skill, but it's fun to play both the melody and the accompaniment of a song on your ukulele.

Some Notes on Strumming

Here are the three basic strumming patterns we will refer to in this book.

- **Strum #1** consists of downward strokes on a steady beat. It's what you feel when you march to a song. When first learning a song, I usually recommend using strum #1 or all-down strums and then later varying the strum to a more challenging one when you've got the chords and melody mastered.

Strum #1

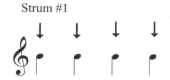

- **Strum #2** consists of even down-up strokes played to a steady beat. It's what classical music sounds like. You play this strum by going down-up-down-up with your fingernails brushing the strings on the down stroke and your thumbnail brushing the strings on the up stroke. This even rhythmic division is called "straight."

Strum #2

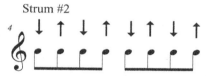

- **Strum #3** consists of down-up strokes to a steady beat, but the down stroke is longer than the up stroke. The rhythm of this strum fits the nursery rhyme "Jack and Jill went up the hill to fetch a pail of water." This uneven division of the beat is called swung. "The Lion Sleeps Tonight" uses a swung rhythmic pattern.

Strum #3

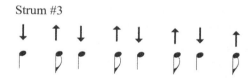

Use the fingernails of your right hand for the down strum and the thumbnail of your right hand for the up strum. Some people also use the pads of their fingers. Do downward strums with the middle three fingers of your right hand. Adjust the angle of your strumming hand so that your fingernails rest gently on String 4, the string closest to the ceiling. Now turn your forearm as if you were rattling a doorknob and allow your fingernails to gently brush down all four strings toward the floor. You may have to experiment to refine your hand shape and the amount of pressure on the strings. Listen to be sure that you are strumming all four strings.

Just in case you were wondering, most uke players do not use a pick because it can break the ukulele's strings. There are felt picks available which will not harm your ukulele's strings.

You should strum across the bottom of the fretboard on the main body of the instrument, NOT where the strings cross over the sound hole in the middle of the instrument. The drawing on the next page shows where your right hand should strum.

Learning these patterns takes time. If your fingers get sore, don't worry. It can take a while to build up thicker skin. We'll suggest some more complicated strumming patterns later in the book that are derived from these three basic patterns.

How to Read Tablature

Lines of the Tab Staff

Each line of the tab staff represents a string on the ukulele. The sounds that are higher in **pitch** are closer to the top of the page just as they are on the standard music **staff**. However, the unfortunate result is that standard tab notation places the lines upside down from how they are arranged on the ukulele.

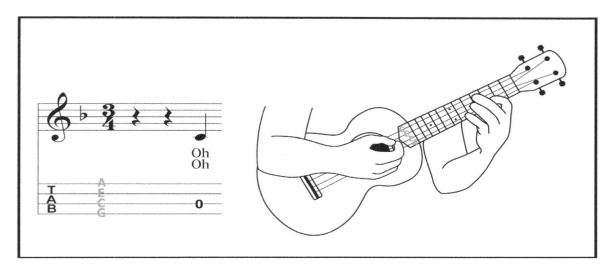

So:

- The top line of the tab staff is the A string (the string closest to the floor when you're playing).
- The line below that is the E string.
- The line below that is the C string.
- The bottom line of the tab is the G string, which is the string closest to the ceiling when you are playing.

Numbers on the Tab Staff

The numbers on the lines of the tab staff tell you which fret to **stop** with a left hand finger. **Stopping** (also called **fretting**) a string means to use a left hand finger and push down firmly so that the string contacts the fret. Your finger goes between the frets, not on a fret.

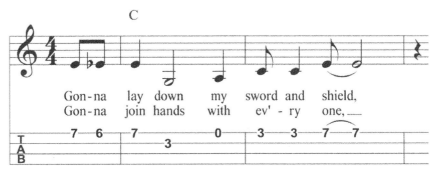

For example, a 5 means to means to put one of your left hand fingers in the fifth fret, and push down on the string as you pluck it with your right hand. A 7 means to stop the string in the 7th fret and pluck it with your right hand. A 4 means to stop the string in the fourth fret and pluck it with your right hand. A 0 means to pluck a string with your right hand without using your left hand at all. We call an unstopped string an *open string*.

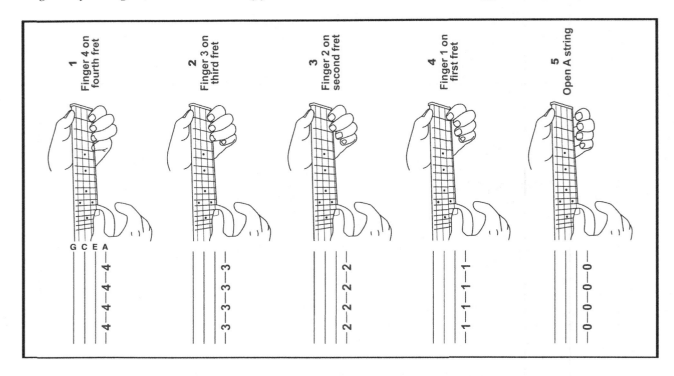

The image above shows a person fretting the A string. Usually we use finger 1 on the first fret, finger 2 on the second fret, finger 3 on the third fret, and finger 4 on the fourth fret. Having your fingers in this arrangement is referred to as *first position*.

For practice reading tab, try playing the sounds shown in the parts of the image. Reading from right to left:

1. Start with finger 4 in the fourth fret and pluck the A string 4 times.
2. Then use finger 3 in the third fret and pluck the A string 4 times.
3. Next use finger 2 in the second fret and pluck the A string 4 times
4. Next use finger 1 in the first fret and pluck the A string 4 times.
5. Finally, pluck the open A string 4 times.

Playing the C Major Scale in Tab Notation

We recommend practicing the C major scale while reading the tab notation as the next step to getting comfortable with reading and playing tab notation. It will help your brain link the look of the tab staff to the muscular patterns needed to play certain notes. Since most melodies are made from fragments of scales, learning this eye-hand coordination will make it a lot easier for you to read tab melodies.

C Major Scale

Putting It Together: Reading a Melody in Tab

Here's an excerpt from our first song, "Lovely Evening." To read the tab, first look at which string line the number is on. Then use your left hand to stop that string in the fret that matches the number shown. Remember that 0 means an open string. We've labeled the lines to make it easier to see which line goes with which string.

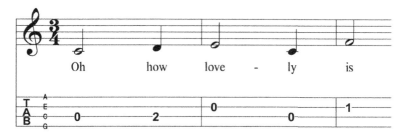

- For the first *note*, don't do anything with your left hand and pluck the C string with your right hand.
- For the second, stop the C string in the second fret.
- For the third note, don't do anything with your left hand and pluck the E string with your right hand.
- For the fourth note, don't do anything with your left hand and pluck the C string with your right hand.
- For the fifth note, stop the E string in the first fret.

Special Lesson Video Format for Tab Melodies

Your free video course has 21 lesson videos, one for each song in the book. Most have a special onscreen format to help you learn tab. As you watch the video lesson, you'll hear the way the music should sound. You'll also see lots of visual cues to help you link how the tab looks with how the music sounds.

Arrow #1 in the screenshot below points to the tab symbol that corresponds to the note you are hearing. In this example it is a 3, circled in red in the video lesson. You'll see Jenny fretting and plucking the string in the main frame of the video. Arrow #2 points at Jenny's finger fretting the string in the first fret.

Arrow #3 points at a dot on the fretboard at the right of the screen. The dot is supposed to represent your finger. It's also supposed to help you see which string and fret go with the tab symbol.

If you think the ukuleles in the lesson videos sound different from yours, it's not your imagination! We are playing tenor ukuleles in the videos, so the G strings are one octave lower than the soprano ukulele that most folks play. Tab staff doesn't show tenor uke's low G because there's no room for it, but as you train your musical ear you'll be able to hear the difference.

How to Tune Your Ukulele

The main thing to know about tuning your ukulele is that you need to compare the sound of the string you are tuning to a source that you know is in tune. For a pitch source you can use a piano, an online tuner, a tuning app, or a clip-on electric tuner.

Your free video course at ukulele.io has a lesson on how to tune your ukulele inside the "Two-Chord Folk Songs" unit. Visit the section of this book called "How to Access Your Free Video Course at ukulele.io" for instructions on how to get to your free course.

Adjust your string to match the sound of the source by turning the tuning peg. Don't worry if you're not sure which way to turn the peg – there are only two directions possible, so experiment until your string sounds like the source.

Which direction to turn the peg depends on how the string was attached to the tuning peg by the person who put the string on your uke, so you have to use your ears to figure it out. One thing remains constant; when the string gets tighter, the pitch (sound) goes up, or higher. When the string gets looser, the pitch goes down.

Be sure to pluck the string as you turn the peg! This will help you hear if the sound is getting higher or lower. Also plucking as you turn will help you avoid tightening the string so much that it breaks.

Once you get your string to match the sound of the tuner, try tuning the string's pitch higher and then lower, just to get more practice listening and turning the tuning peg at the same time.

By the way, it's best to first tune your string's pitch slightly lower than the target pitch and then gradually adjust it back up until it matches. As you lower the string's pitch, you're loosening the tension on the string. Then pluck as you turn the peg to adjust the pitch from slightly too low to perfectly in tune.

Tuning this way will help the tension above the tuning peg nut to equal the tension on the instrument's neck. This will help keep the string in tune longer – always a good thing! Don't worry if you didn't understand this last paragraph; as you get more experience tuning your ukulele, you'll understand better how it works.

Fingerpicking Technique

Jenny uses two different ways of *fingerpicking* the melodies of the songs.

- **Plucking with your index finger:** use this method for a faster moving song. Put your right thumb against the edge of the *fretboard* and pluck with your right index finger, pulling the string toward the ceiling to make the sound. This method will give you more rhythmic control and let you play faster.
- **Plucking with your thumb:** use this method for a slower moving song. This method will give you a richer sound.

As you work your way through the book, we'll teach you how to fingerpick chords one note at a time (called "broken" chords). We'll also teach you two techniques for quick moving melody notes. One is called a "hammer on" and the other is called a "pull-off."

One Last Thing: Be Sure to Sign Up for Your Free Video Course!

With purchase of this book you get access to a video course hosted at ukulele.io as a free goodie. Watching the video lessons can make learning the ukulele easier and more fun, so we hope you'll sign up. As the old saying goes, a picture is worth a thousand words, and a video is probably worth a lot more.

In the back of the book is a section with step by step instructions and screenshots to show you how to access your free course at our website, ukulele.io. Or you can visit ukulele.io/access-free-video-course. We're so convinced of the learning value of the video course that we will be happy to set up your account for you. Just shoot us an email at ukulele.io/contact-us/.

> If you're thinking, "Why should I be bothered to sign up for the course when I already have the book?" check out what some other customers have to say:
>
> "You can watch and play along with the video and sound tracks. All the learning procedures are set out to keep you happy, as you watch, listen and learn to play. It's an excellent tutorial programme."
>
> "The videos are charmingly amateurish in a way that makes me think "I can do it too"."
>
> "Between this book and the associated video tutorials, I learned so much so quickly. I was able to pick out some songs (on my ukulele) the first day I messed around with it."

Two-Chord Folk Songs

The question of exactly what a folk song is has many different answers. We've gone with Google's definition: music that originates in traditional popular culture or that is written in such a style. So you'll find songs in this book whose composers are known as well as songs whose origins are lost in the past.

We've included versions of "Lovely Evening" and "Lil' Liza Jane" in the keys of F and C. Both songs are easier to play in the key of C, and easier for most folks to sing in the key of F. We've assumed you already know how to play these chords:

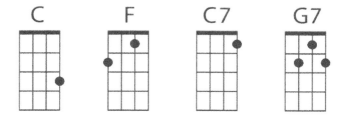

If you are new to the ukulele, we suggest starting with "Lil' Liza Jane" in the key of F. To play the song in F you'll need the F and the C7 chord. Once you are comfortable with the song in F, try it in C. To play the song in C you'll need the C and G7 chords. G7 is a harder chord for most people because it uses three fingers.

How to Play the B Flat Major Chord

As you can see from the photograph, you will need to put your first finger on two strings at once to master this chord. Experiment with different finger angles and pressures to make sure your first finger is fretting two strings at once. You might try practicing just the first finger position by itself until it is comfortable, or at least sounding good, and then try adding the other fingers.

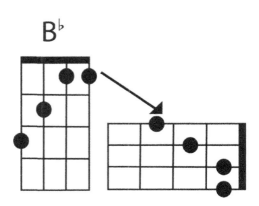

Using one finger to stop more than one string at a time is a technique used in another type of ukulele chord called a **barre chord**. While learning this skill can be challenging, the advantage of a barre chord is that you can move it to different frets to get lots of different chords from one hand shape.

Lovely Evening

As previously mentioned, you'll see versions of "Lovely Evening" in the keys of C and F. "Lovely Evening" in F uses the B flat chord, which is one of the hardest three-finger ukulele chords. It is a commonly used chord, so it's best to master it. If you are struggling to play this chord, you might want to play only the C major version of "Lovely Evening." You can always come back to the F major version later. The E minor chord (see the chapter on "Minor Mode") will help you learn the B flat chord shape.

"Lovely Evening" is a German folk song. It's usually sung as a **round**. Bing Crosby recorded the song in a medley on his 1961 album "101 Gang Songs." The music sounds very calm because there are only two chords. There's also a feeling of gentle swaying created by the use of three beats per **measure.**

This section is left blank for your notes

Strumming Pattern:
↓　↓　↓

Lovely Evening

Strumming Pattern:
↓ ↓ ↓

Lovely Evening

Lil' Liza Jane

"Lil' Liza Jane" is a song dating back to the beginning of the 20th century. It's become a standard, not only in New Orleans Jazz, but also in folk music, bluegrass, and rock and roll. It is one of the most recognized songs in the world, which makes for a perfect sing-along.

A 1918 book by Natalie Curtis Burlin titled "Negro Folk-Songs" documents a dancing game played to this song. Couples dance in a circle around a man in the middle who has no partner. He does a solo dance until he can steal a partner from the circle of couples. The man who has lost his partner now dances in the middle until he can steal a new one.

As with "Lovely Evening" you'll see versions of "Lil' Liza Jane" in keys of C and F. A chord melody or solo ukulele version in the key of F is also included for "Lil' Liza Jane" where you can play both the melody and the accompaniment on your ukulele.

This section is left blank for your notes

Strumming Pattern:
↓ ↓↑ ↓ ↓↑

Lil' Liza Jane

Lil' Liza Jane

Chord Melody

Strumming Pattern:

Lil' Liza Jane

Three-Chord Folk Songs

For the four songs in this chapter in C major, you'll need the first three chords shown below:

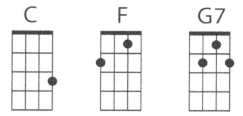

We've also included versions of two of the songs in F: "Happy Birthday" and "Go Tell Aunt Rhody." For these two songs you'll need these chords:

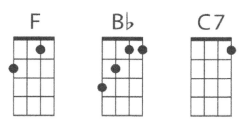

<u>**This section is left blank for your notes**</u>

Happy Birthday

"Happy Birthday" is the most recognized song in the English language, at least according to the 1998 Guinness World Records. For many years, Warner/Chappell Music claimed the song was copyrighted and collected about $2 million annually in royalties. In 2015 a federal judge ruled that the company's claim of copyright was invalid and this famous song happily entered the public domain.

You'll see versions of "Happy Birthday" in the key of C and key of F.

Happy Birthday in C

Happy Birthday in F

Strumming Pattern:
↓   ↓   ↓

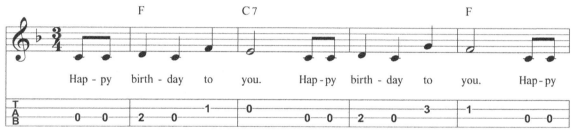

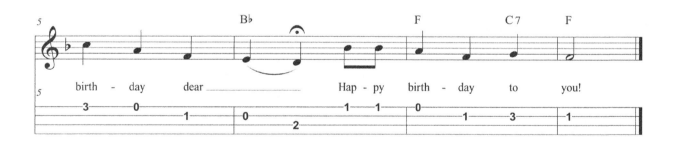

Go Tell Aunt Rhody

The melody of "Go Tell Aunt Rhody" was originally a dance tune in a 1752 opera written by the French 18th century philosopher Jean-Jacques Rousseau. The tune became popular in England and America and was published with a variety of different lyrics.

We have included versions of "Go Tell Aunt Rhody" in the keys of C and F as well as a chord melody arrangement in the key of F.

Strumming Pattern:
↓ ↓↑ ↓ ↓↑

Go Tell Aunt Rhody in F

Go Tell Aunt Rhody

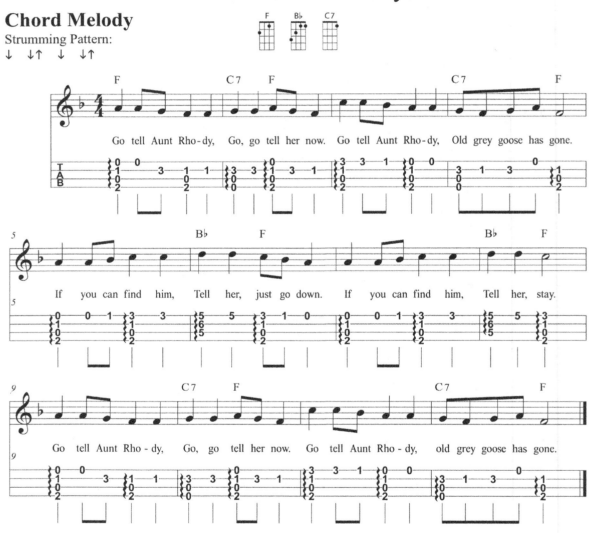

Wabash Cannonball

The "Wabash Cannonball" is the oldest song on the Rock and Roll Hall of Fame's list of *500 Songs that Shaped Rock and Roll*. It's about an express train which traveled throughout the middle and western United States in the late 1800s and early 1900s. Many artists have recorded the song, including the Carter Family, Roy Acuff, Woody Guthrie, and Johnny Cash.

This section is left blank for your notes

Strumming Pattern:
↓ ↓↑ ↓ ↓↑

Wabash Cannonball

Verses:

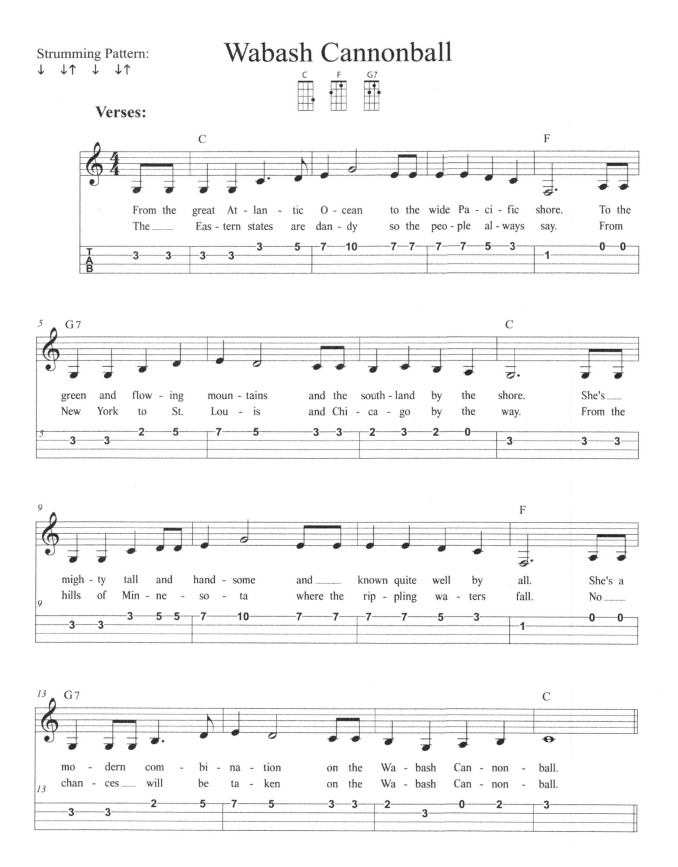

Chorus:

Lis - ten to the jin - gle, the ___ rum - ble and the roar. As she

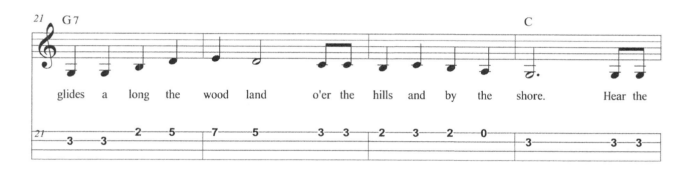

glides a - long the wood - land o'er the hills and by the shore. Hear the

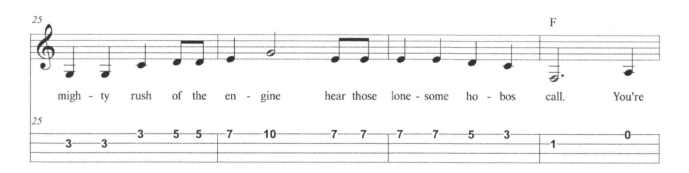

migh - ty rush of the en - gine hear those lone - some ho - bos call. You're

trav - e - ling through the jun - gle on the Wa - bash Can - non - ball.

Big Rock Candy Mountain

"Big Rock Candy Mountain" is a well known American folk song about a hobo who describes a paradise on Earth to a boy. Like Honaloochie and Sukarita, the Big Rock Candy Mountain originally was a mythical place. However, several places have been named after the song, including some hills near Marysvale, Utah.

Strumming Pattern:
↓ ↓↑ ↓ ↓↑

Three-Chord Blues Songs

A Very Brief Introduction to the Blues

Blues is a uniquely American style of folk music that originated in the African American communities of the southern U.S. around the turn of the century. Many elements of the blues can be traced back to the music of Africa. Most American popular music grew out of the blues.

The blues uses a 12-measure chord progression consisting of chords that have a specific pitch spacing and relationship to one another. ("*Bar*" is another word for "*measure.*") The simplest form of 12-bar blues uses the *chord progression* below. Each letter stands for a measure of music.

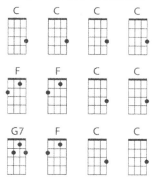

Songs that use the 12-bar blues often have a section where one musician makes up new melodies while others continue to play the 12-bar blues progression. Blues melodies are always made from a specific family of notes called the *blues scale*. That's what makes them sound "bluesy."

It can be fun to try your hand at blues improvisation using a recording to play along with. You can find one here: goo.gl/AgTBLH. If you're interested in learning more about blues improvisation, visit ukulele.io/21MOREprint to check out our book *21 More Songs in 6 Days: Learn Intermediate Ukulele the Easy Way.*

Worried Man Blues

The origins of "Worried Man Blues" are lost in the mists of the 19th century. Its famous opening line, "It takes a worried man to sing a worried song," was popularized on records in 1930, when it was recorded by the Carter Family. It was also recorded by Woody Guthrie and the Kingston Trio, and in 2001 it was used as the theme song for the PBS series *American Roots Music*.

"Worried Man Blues" has a 16-bar verse and chorus, rather than the 12 bars most often used by blues songs. It is usually performed with the chorus alternating with the verses. Some versions of this song have many verses which tell a detailed story of waking up to discover that you've been sentenced to working on a railroad for 21 years. We've included three verses here – hopefully enough to convey a condensed version of the story.

Worried Man Blues

Strumming Pattern:
↓ ↓↑ ↓ ↓↑

Verses:

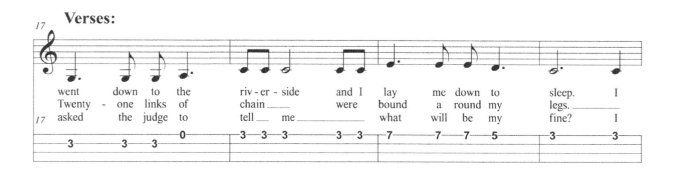

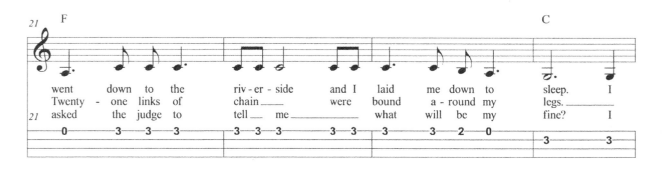

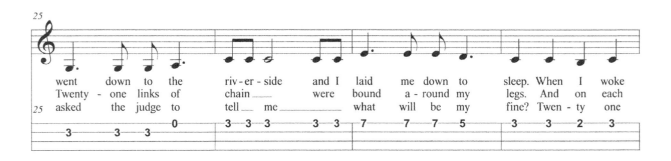

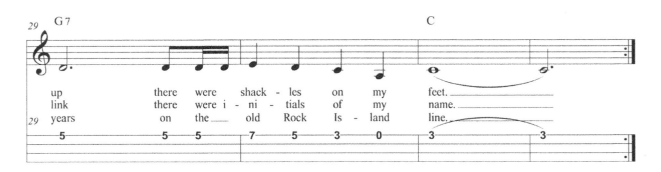

St. Louis Blues

"St. Louis Blues" was composed in 1914 by W.C. Handy. It was one of the first blues songs to succeed as a popular song and has remained a jazz standard. It was also a long term success, earning Handy $25,000 per year in royalties as late as 1958 – that's over $200,000 in today's dollars. "St. Louis Blues" is in a standard 12-bar blues form, and is organized verse, verse, then chorus.

Four-Chord Folk Songs

To play the songs in this chapter, you will need these four chords:

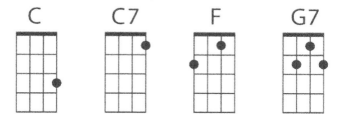

Goodnight, Irene

The exact origins of "Goodnight, Irene" are not known. The famous folk song researchers John and Alan Lomax recorded American blues musician Huddie "Lead Belly" Ledbetter singing it in 1933. Later covers of the song by The Weavers and Frank Sinatra became huge hits.

This section is left blank for your notes

Goodnight, Irene

Down by the Riverside

"Down by the Riverside" is an African American **spiritual** and **work song** from the 19th century. It's also known by the title "Ain't Gonna Study War No More." The song's central image about casting off aggression and putting on spiritual garb at the side of the river has several meanings. It refers to baptism and to going to heaven after death. It also could be interpreted as a reference to escaping slavery, with the river in the song being the Ohio River which was the border between slave and free states before the American Civil War.

This section is left blank for your notes

Down by the Riverside

Strumming Pattern:
↓ ↓↑ ↑↓↑

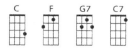

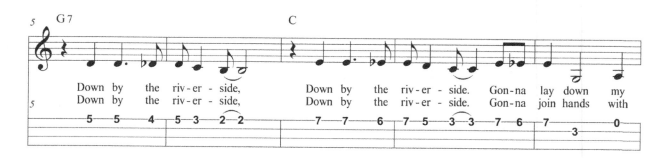

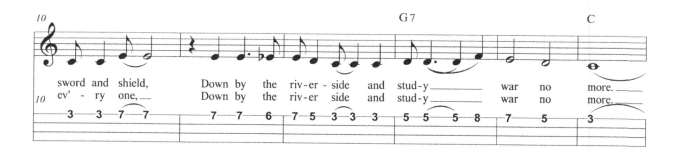

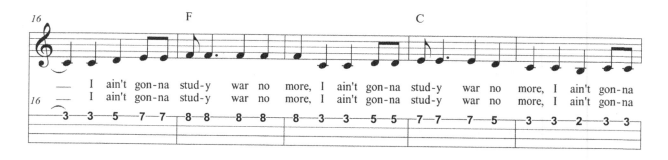

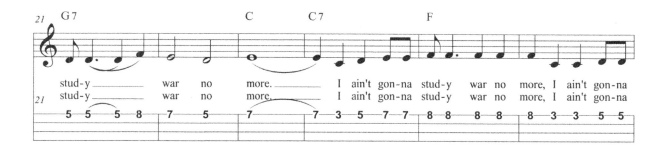

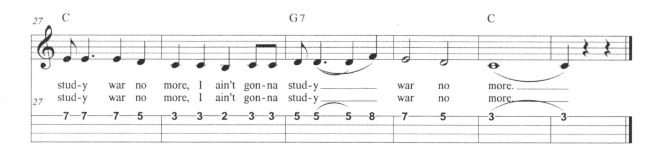

Minor Mode

So far all the songs in this book have been in what musicians call major – C major, to be precise. The songs in this chapter will be in minor modes (mode is another word for scale). Most people hear minor mode as darker or perhaps sadder or more mysterious.

Because these songs use a different scale, they also use different chords. That's because the notes of a scale are used to build its chords. If you would like to know more about scales and chords and how they relate to one another, you will enjoy our book *21 More Songs in 6 Days: Learn Intermediate Ukulele the Easy Way*.

How to Play the A Minor, D Minor and E7 Chords

Here are the chords used in this chapter's songs. Notice the lower case 'm' next to the capital letters A and D? It stands for 'minor'.

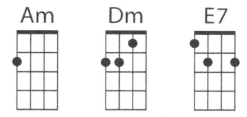

A minor is an easier version of the F major chord. Simply omit the first finger in the first fret.

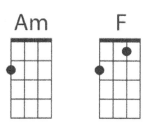

47

D minor is also close to the F chord shape. One way to play this chord is to use the same fingers in the same frets as for the F chord, and simply flatten your second finger slightly so that it stops two strings rather than one.

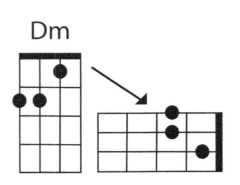
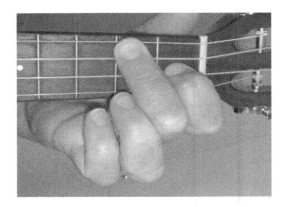

You could also play the D minor chord using three fingers.

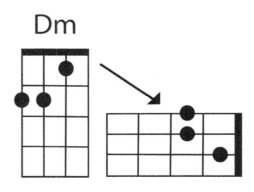

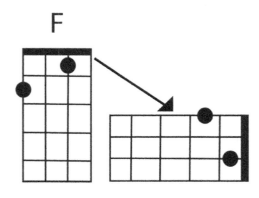
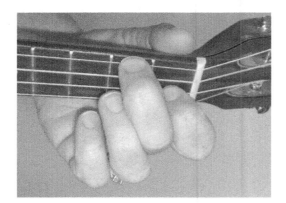

Finally, here's the symbol and photo for the **E7 chord**.

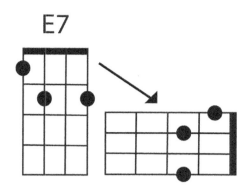 

Sometimes I Feel Like a Motherless Child

"Sometimes I Feel Like a Motherless Child" is a traditional African American spiritual which dates back to the era of slavery in the United States. It has many variations and has been recorded by many different artists. The lyrics express the pain and despair of a child who has lost its mother.

This section is left blank for your notes

Sometimes I Feel Like a Motherless Child

Sakura

Even though "Sakura" is in minor, its message is joyful. "Sakura" is a traditional Japanese folk song about the cherry tree, which represents beauty, peace and joy in the Japanese culture. Its blooming heralds the arrival of spring and is associated with renewal and rebirth. The song refers to "hanami," or blossom viewing, which is a traditional springtime pastime in Japan.

A chord melody arrangement is included for "Sakura" so you can play the melody and the accompaniment at the same time.

Chord Melody:

Strumming Pattern:

↓ ↓ ↓ ↓

Sakura

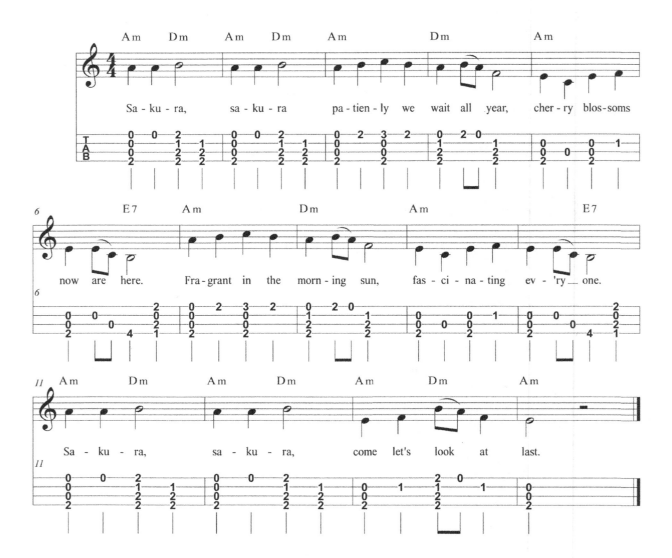

Five-Chord Folk Songs

Here are the chords you will need for the songs in this chapter. The chords that are new to this chapter are G, E minor, F minor and D7.

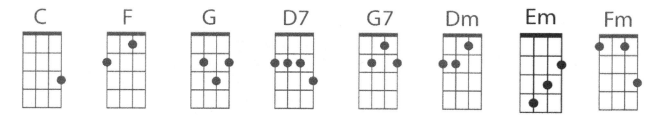

How to Play the E Minor, F Minor, and G Chords

For the E minor chord, think of making a diagonal line with your left hand fingers on the fret board. We've also included an alternate two-finger version of the E minor chord in the Chord Glossary at the back of the book.

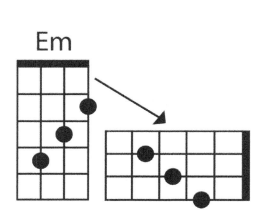

For both the F minor and G major chords, you will place fingers 1 and 2 one string apart. For the G major chord, place fingers 1 and 2 in the second fret. Then reach with your third finger to the third fret.

For the F minor chord place fingers 1 and 2 in the first fret. Then reach finger 4 to the third fret. While many people feel less comfortable with finger 4 than with finger 3, most people cannot stretch finger 3 to the third fret with fingers 1 and 2 both in the first fret.

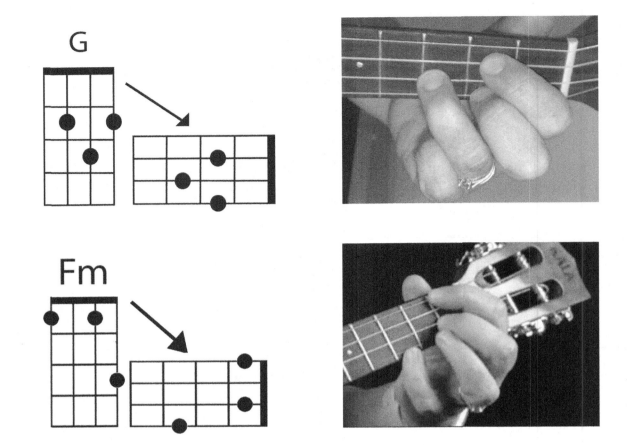

How to Play the D7 Chord

"Easy" or "Hawaiian" D7

The first version of D7 only uses two fingers. Using this version of D7 makes it much easier to switch to the three finger G chord because the D7 shape is closely related to the G shape. Both shapes use fingers 1 and 2 one string apart.

The D7 chord is also musically very closely is that related to the G chord, so they often show up close to one another in music. D7 is an important member of the family of chords that belong to the G major scale: the dominant seventh (V7) chord. You can learn all about dominants, scales and chords in our book *21 More Ukulele Songs in 6 Days: Learn Intermediate Ukulele the Easy Way.*

D7

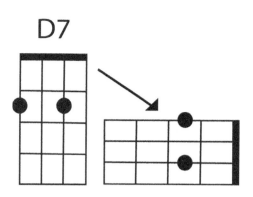

Movable Barre D7

The second version of D7 also uses only two fingers, but you have to flatten a finger in the second fret so you are stopping three strings with one finger. It can take quite a bit of practice to get comfortable with this flattened finger position, which is referred to as a ***barre*** (or "bar"). The big plus of the D7 barre chord shape is that you can then slide your left hand up and down the fret board and play lots of other similar sounding dominant 7th chords using the same hand shape. Ukulele players refer to this type of chord as a "movable barre" chord.

D7

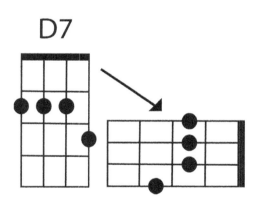

All Through the Night

"All Through the Night" is a Welsh lullaby first notated by Edward Jones in 1784. The tune has been used for a number of Christian hymns and is sometimes considered a Christmas song.

Molly Malone

"Molly Malone" is sometimes also referred to as "Cockles and Mussels." While there is no hard evidence that the song is Irish, it is considered the unofficial anthem of the city of Dublin, Ireland. In 1988, a statue of Molly Malone was placed on one of Dublin's main streets.

Beautiful Dreamer

"Beautiful Dreamer" was composed by Stephen Foster in 1864 near the end of his life. He was poor and in bad health, and survived by writing songs quickly and selling them at very low prices. Other songs by Stephen Foster include "Oh Susannah," "Old Folks at Home," and "Camptown Races."

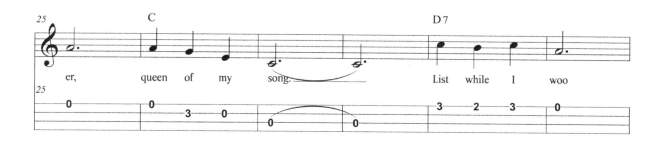

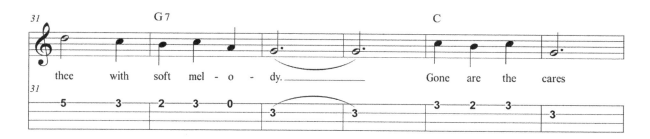

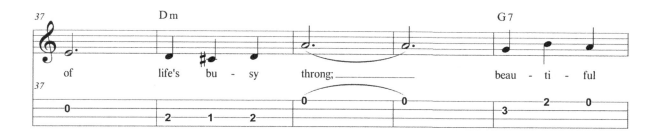

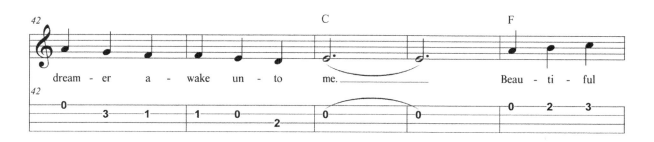

Shenandoah

"Shenandoah" is a traditional American folk song which was widely popular in the 19th century. American folk song researcher Alan Lomax felt that it was a work song sung by French-Canadian fur traders. Others think that it is of Native American origin because its lyrics tell the story of Sally, the daughter of chief Shenandoah. Still others think the song is about the Shenandoah River.

We've included tab showing how to accompany the melody by *fingerpicking broken* chords.

This section is left blank for your notes

Shenandoah

Strumming Pattern:
↓ ↓ ↓ ↓ or
↓ ↓↑ ↓ ↓↑

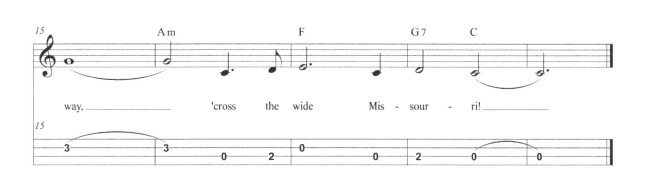

Shenandoah with Accompaniment

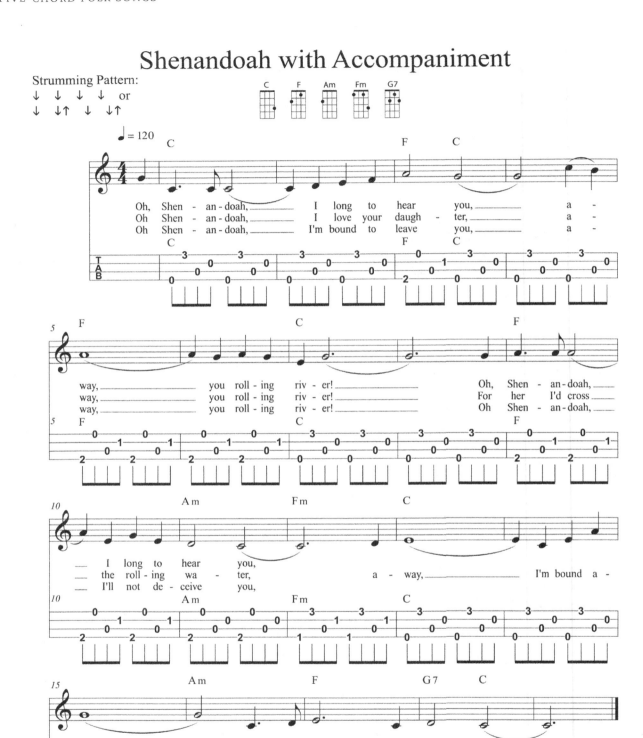

Six-Chord Folk Songs

Here are the chords you will need for the songs in this chapter.

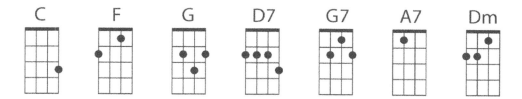

The new chord for this chapter is A7 – an easy one-finger chord.

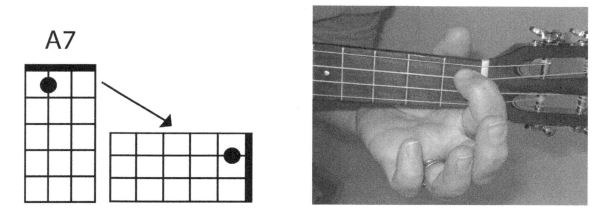

The Ash Grove

"The Ash Grove" is a traditional Welsh folk melody that has been paired with many different lyrics. The best known version was written by Thomas Oliphant. The tune has also been used by many hymns. We've included tab showing how to accompany the melody by fingerpicking broken chords.

The Ash Grove

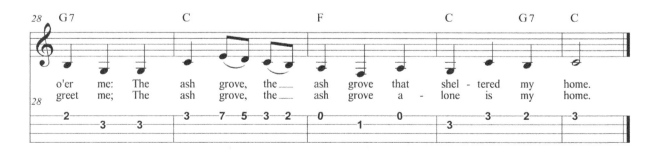

The Ash Grove Accompaniment

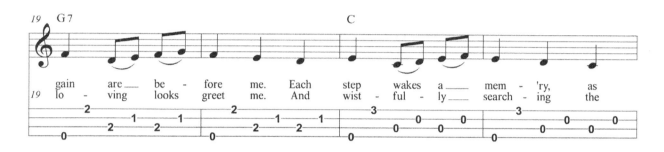

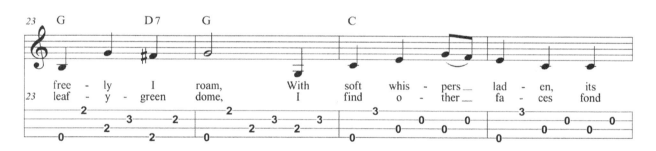

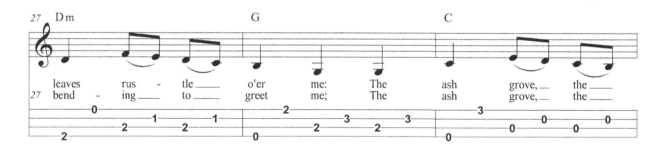

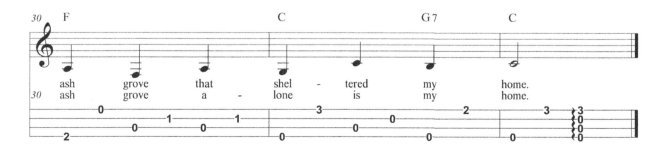

Take Me Out to the Ball Game

"Take Me Out to the Ball Game" was composed in 1908 by Jack Norworth and Albert Von Tilzer, neither of who had ever attended a baseball game before writing the song. It's become the unofficial anthem of North American baseball and is usually sung during the middle of the seventh inning of a game.

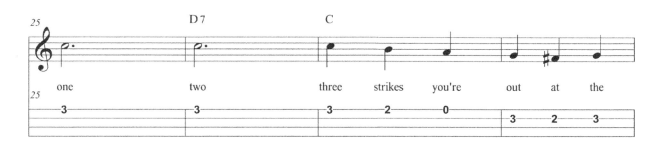

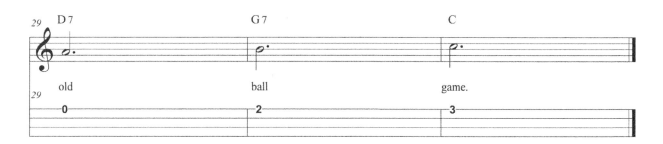

Folk Songs in G Major

The chords for the songs in this chapter are:

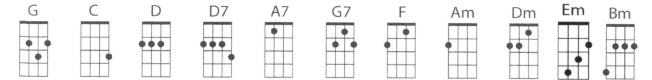

So far in this book all the songs have been in the key of C. C major is the most ukulele friendly key because the four open strings of the ukulele are tuned to *pitches* of the C scale. That means that when playing in C you encounter chords which use more open strings and fewer fingers. Now we are venturing into the scale of G major. You'll be able to play the songs in this chapter with the chords you've used so far, with the exception of one new chord:

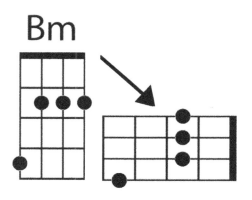

Turkey in the Straw

"Turkey in the Straw" is an American folk tune dating from the early 19ᵗʰ century. Originally a fiddle tune, minstrel shows popularized it as a song. There are many different versions of the lyrics. According to survivors, it was one of the songs played by the band during the sinking of the *Titanic*. It is also part of the soundtrack of *Steamboat Willie*, a famous early Mickey Mouse cartoon.

We've included both a vocal version with lyrics and an instrumental version. While this song has only three chords, it is usually played at a fast tempo which will require your left hand to be very comfortable with changing between the G and D7 chords. If you are lucky enough to have a friend that plays fiddle, you can strum the chords while your friend plays the melody.

Strumming Pattern:

Turkey in the Straw

Strumming Pattern:
↓ ↓↑ ↓ ↓↑

Turkey in the Straw-Instrumental

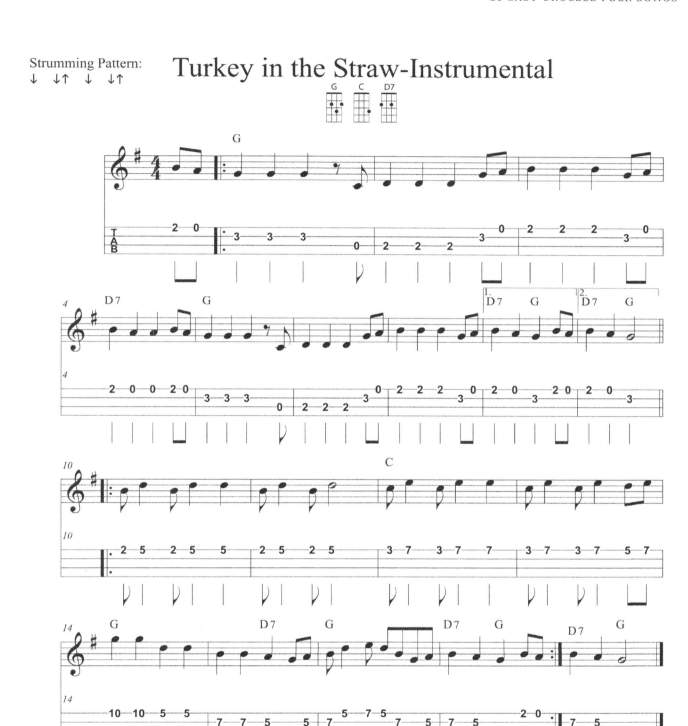

My Bonnie Lies Over the Ocean

"My Bonnie Lies Over the Ocean" is a traditional Scottish folk song. Like many folk songs, its origin is unknown. Some think it may refer to Charles Edward Stuart (1720-1788), known as Bonnie Prince Charlie. After the Prince's defeat by the English at the Battle of Culloden, his supporters could have sung this song in his honor. It was published in 1870 and became popular on college campuses and for group singing.

My Bonnie Lies Over the Ocean

Sweet Betsy from Pike

"Sweet Betsy from Pike" is an American ballad that tells the story of a frontier woman named Betsy and her lover Ike. They travel from Pike County (probably in Missouri) to California. Because the terms "Betsy" and "Old Betsy" were common frontier nicknames for rifles, scholar John Ciardi has theorized that the song was originally a comic tribute to a rifle. Our version begins in the key of G and then uses three chords (D minor, G7 and C) to transition to the key of C. If you wanted to, you could play the entire song in either G or C.

This section is left blank for your notes

Strum pattern:

↓ ↓↑ ↓

Sweet Betsy from Pike

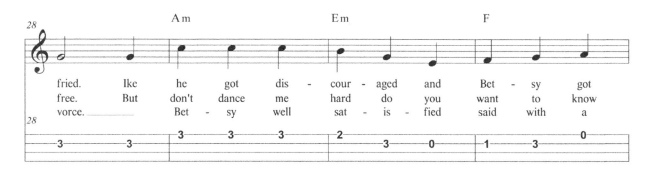

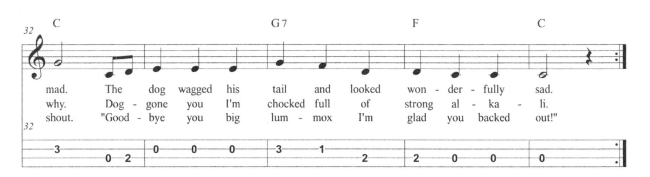

Enjoying This Book? You Can Make a Difference

Reviews are one of the most powerful marketing tools an author has. Honest reviews can help bring this book to the attention of other ukulele players who would benefit from it.

If you have enjoyed this book and found it helpful, Jenny and I would be very grateful if you could spend a few minutes leaving a short review on our book's Amazon page.

You can get there easily by typing ukulele.io/folkreview into your browser window.

Thank you so much for your time and your help. We wish you a lifetime of happiness making music.

Jenny Peters and Rebecca Bogart
The Ukulele Sisters

How to Access Your Free Video Course at ukulele.io

     You get a free video course because you bought this book. Follow the directions below or visit this page for a video and the most up-to-date instructions on how to access your course.

> ukulele.io/access-free-video-course

Keeping our instructions up to date online instead of in print frees up time for us to create more books and courses for you. If you have any trouble, please drop us a note at ukulele.io/contact-us/. We want you to start enjoying your free course as soon as possible!

Here's What to Do

1. **Go to this secret link.**

> ukulele.io/folksongs

Or you can scan the following QR Code:

2. You will see the page shown below. **Enter your email address in the box and click the green button that says "Submit".**

3. **Check your inbox** for an email from us. Click the link in the email. You'll be taken to a shopping cart in our store.

4. You'll see a video course in the cart discounted 100% so that you pay nothing. **Enter the details under "Customer Information."** If you already have an account at ukulele.io, you'll need to login first before placing your order.

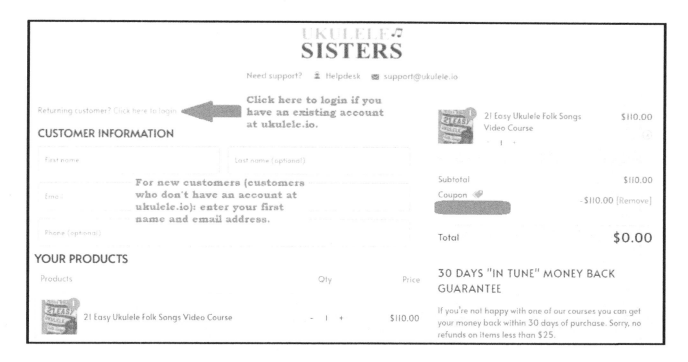

If you have an existing account at ukulele.io and you clicked the "Click here to login link," you'll see the following screen. Enter your username (or email) and password and click the "Login" button.

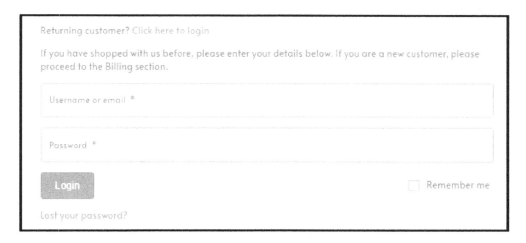

Once you've logged in (for returning customers) or entered the details under "Customer Information" (for new customers), scroll down and **click the green "Place Order Now" button.**

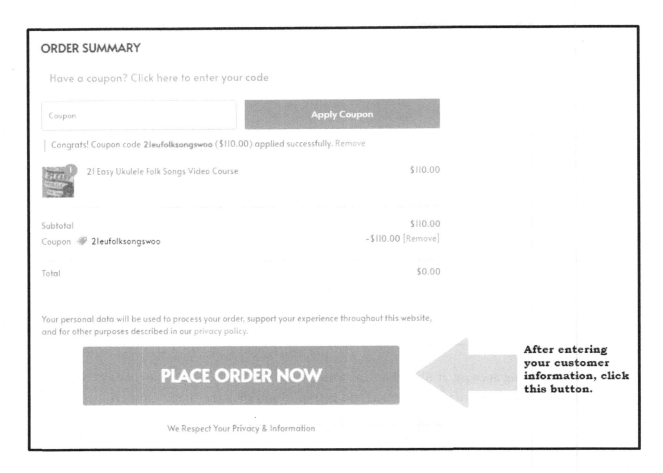

5. After you click "Place Order" you'll see this page. **Click on the link in the first line that says 'go to your courses page'.**

6. Click on your course name to display the lesson names. Click on any lesson name to get to your course pages. Enjoy!

7. If you are new to ukulele.io, **check your email** for a message from us with your username and password so you can log in for later sessions. If you already have an account at ukulele.io, you will not receive an email as you can continue to use your current username and password.

What If I Already Have an Account at ukulele.io?

Go ahead and enter your email at ukulele.io/folksongs. Then go through each step above so that you 'purchase' the course that goes with this book using the 100% off coupon.

Just a heads up: you won't get an email from us with your username and password because you can use your current username and password. If you've forgotten your password, go to ukulele.io/my-account/ and click on 'Lost your password?' to reset your password.

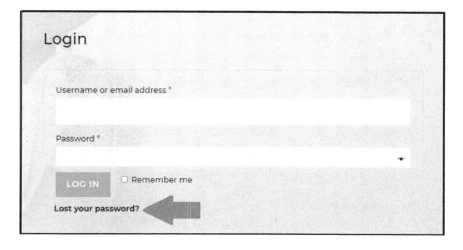

How to Sign In to Your Free Video Course at ukulele.io

Once you've signed up for your course using the secret link above, you can log in from the home page of ukulele.io for future practice sessions. Here's how.

1. Hover over "Sign In to Access Video Lessons" in the upper right corner of your screen. **Click on "My Account"** from the drop down menu that appears.

If you don't see the "Sign In" option, scroll right or enlarge your browser window until it appears. Or go directly to:

ukulele.io/my-account/

Enter your username and password then click the "LOG IN" button.

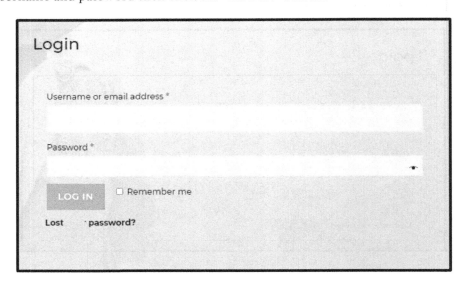

2. You will be taken to this page. **Click on 'Courses'.**

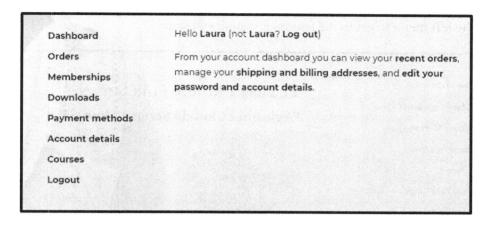

3. **Click on your course name** or the triangle in front of it. The names of the units will show up.

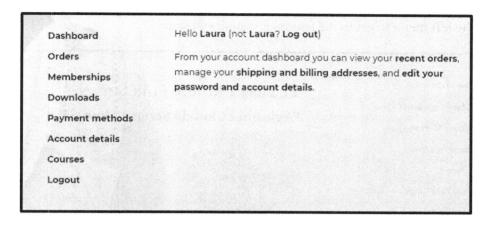

4. **Click on a lesson name** to get to the lesson pages.

5. **Click on the left menu** to get to the lesson or course you want.

21 Easy Ukulele Folk Songs
Beginning Ukulele Songs Volume 5

Here's where you'll access the lesson videos that go with *21 Easy Ukulele Folk Songs*. We hope you'll visit often.

v02162024

Get the Rest of the Beginning Ukulele Songs Series!

One of our books can help you move to the next level with your playing no matter where you are in your ukulele journey. All feature detailed and easy-to-follow instructions. We pick songs and carefully put them in an order that will help you build up gradually to more difficult skills. With our approach you'll continue to improve your playing without getting frustrated or developing bad habits.

Each is available in both paper and eBook versions and comes with its own companion video course at ukulele.io.

Book 1: 21 Songs in 6 Days: Learn Ukulele the Easy Way

Learn the five easiest ukulele chords (C, Am, F, C7, and G7) and three basic strums. Learn to change chords while keeping a steady strum going. By the end of the book you'll be playing five-chord songs. Book purchase includes a 101-minute video course to help you learn faster.

Get your copy at ukulele.io/Buy21Songs.

I could not have asked for a better way to learn the ukulele!! Pairing the book with the online video lessons was the perfect way for me to learn! I felt like I was having my own private lesson.

I can't wait to move onto the next book and keep learning! I have not been able to sing with my church choir nor ring in our bell choir, with everything that has happened. Music is cathartic for me and I am extremely thankful for my ukulele, which oddly enough I just had laying around, and for your books and videos. You have been a life saver!!

Thank you!!!

Daisy Richardson

Book 2: Easy Ukulele Songs: Five with Five Chords

Hone your ability to change chords by playing five favorite five-chord songs. Learn four more easy chords. Learn fancier strumming patterns that combine the 3 basic strums from Book 1. Also get more practice with harder tab melodies and an introduction to the blues and blues improvisation in the key of C. Comes with 10 video free course to help you learn the songs.

Get your copy at ukulele.io/5x5.

Total ukulele beginner. I enjoyed this work. It takes the skills learned in book 1 to a new level. I enjoyed a couple of the songs, especially "Five Foot Two." It's nice to find 1920s style songs because they are so naturally ukulele songs. I also enjoyed "Greensleeves" because the ukulele sounds more lute-like. The pedagogical learning approach is cool, thoughtful, and systematic. An excellent series. I bought this after reviewing other ukulele learning methods online and trying others from the library.

Book 3: 21 Easy Ukulele Songs for Christmas

21 seasonal favorites arranged in order of difficulty. After learning one new chord (D minor), you'll be able to play every song in the book with the chords you learned in Book 2 of the series. Get more practice reading tab melodies and using a variety of strumming patterns. The free course that comes with your book has a lesson video for every song in the book. Great for caroling or playing duets with fellow uke lovers.

Get your copy at ukulele.io/xmasnow.

I have purchased both the 21 songs in 6 days and the Christmas one. I have never picked up an Instrument in my 48 years of being on this earth and these books are making everything so easy to learn and are a lot of fun!!! THANK YOU!!!!!

You sure can use my name!

Scott Harkema

Book 4: 21 MORE Easy Ukulele Songs: Learn Intermediate Ukulele the Easy Way

Learn the most important intermediate ukulele chords. If you've been working your way through the Beginning Ukulele Songs series, you'll learn five new chords, including the including the dreaded B flat chord: D, E minor, B flat, G minor, and C major 7.

You'll get more practice fingerpicking melodies and learn how to fingerpick accompaniments too. We'll introduce new fancier strumming patterns, songs in minor mode, and songs with three beats per measure. And get more practice with the blues by playing more difficult blues songs in a variety of keys. Finally, you'll learn how to play great ukulele solo (chord melody) arrangements of several songs.

All songs include both a standard music staff and tab notation, and several strumming patterns. The accompanying free course includes 40+ lesson videos.

Get your copy at ukulele.io/21MOREprint.

I thought you may like to know, I am joining my Ukulele group for a performance in a local village Hall, early in November. It may not be the greatest achievement ever, but I am looking forward to the show. Rest assured without the help of your books and videos, this experience would have been beyond me, thank you for helping have such fun.

Roy C. Edwards

Book 6: 21 Easy Ukulele Hymns

22 favorite hymns arranged in order of difficulty. The book begins with fourteen 2 and 3 chord hymns and includes favorites such as "Amazing Grace," "Be Thou My Vision," "Nearer My God to Thee" and "Fairest Lord Jesus." Many hymns are presented in 2 keys so you can choose a comfortable key for singing or playing. There's melody tab and a suggested strumming pattern for every hymn. Get your copy at ukulele.io/hymns.

Check out our Hymn Kits at ukulele.io/hymnkits to get access to a 210-minute video course plus 13 chord melody hymn arrangements and bonus hymns.

I have been anxiously awaiting this book becoming available and it has been worth the wait. I received mine yesterday, and found myself going back to play songs out of it multiple times throughout the day. I love all the variety to the different ways to play the many songs-picking, strums, different keys. Playing these wonderful old hymns will bring hours of joy to my life, and I look forward to picking up extra tips from the video tutorials. I definitely would recommend adding this book to your ukulele music collection.

Janet Wentz

Other Courses That Work Great with Your Book

Do a deeper dive into various ukulele topics with our online courses and kits.

Learn Easy Ukulele Chord Melody Today!

Get everything you need to know to start playing chord melody at an easy level with this exciting course. If you can play the songs in our books, you can learn easy ukulele chord melody with this course. Find out more at ukulele.io/EasyChordMelody.
- Learn to play chords and melody at the same time for a beautiful 'solo ukulele' sound.
- Don't want to sing? This is the perfect course for you!

Easy Ukulele Hymn Kits

With a Hymn Kit you'll get:
- a 45+ video course to help you learn the hymns.
- sheet music for tags and turnarounds so you can connect your hymns together.
- fabulous solo ukulele arrangements of hymns so you can play the melody and accompaniment yourself.

Available in Regular and Premium versions. Find out more at ukulele.io/21-easy-ukulele-hymns-is-here/.

Practice Makes Permanent Program

Do you want to learn how to practice better? Do you struggle with singing and strumming at the same time? Or, do you struggle with changing chords? Does fingerpicking sound cool, but it seems hard?

When you get our "Practice Makes Permanent Program," you learn how to practice. You make a deep dive into real improvement and a commitment to playing the ukulele well. You get an online membership that gives you weekly practice guidance. You improve on your ukulele. And you do it with a group of people who come together in a closed Facebook group.

You get:
- Practice charts and suggestions to organize your practicing
- Questions for reflection
- Membership in a closed Facebook Group to build community
- Periodic video updates that address questions from members

The program starts at the beginning of our first book, *21 Songs in 6 Days*, and moves through the next four books. Book 6, *21 Easy Ukulele Hymns*, has its separate course - see "Easy Ukulele Hymn Kits." Along the way you learn the underlying musical skills of each song. You turbocharge your practice.

Learn more about this program at ukulele.io/permanent-program-basp-new/.

Chord Glossary

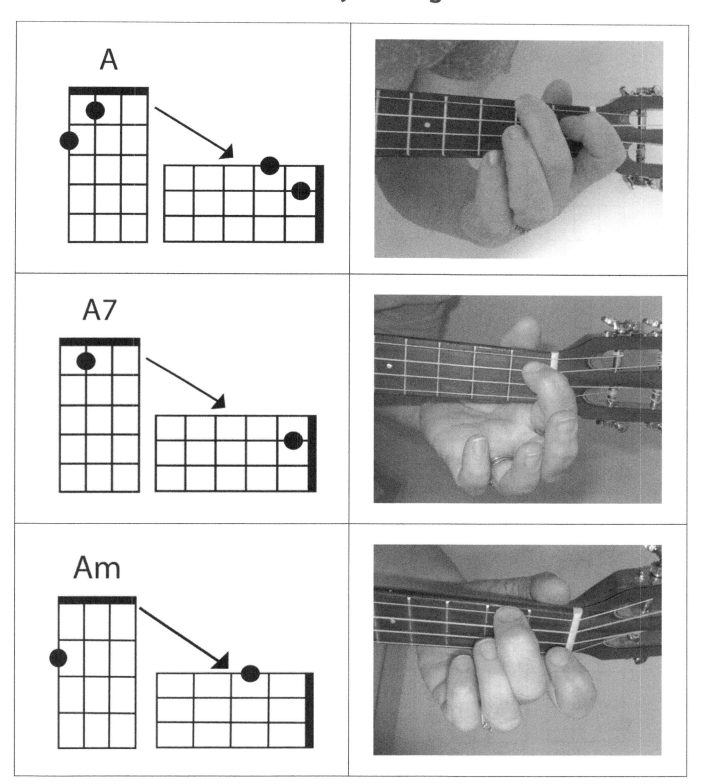

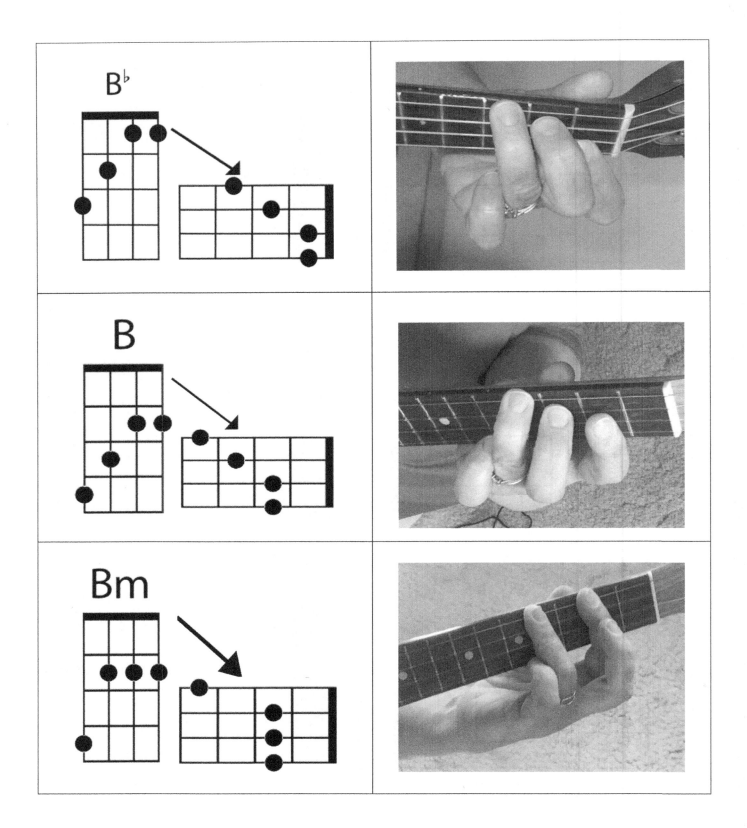

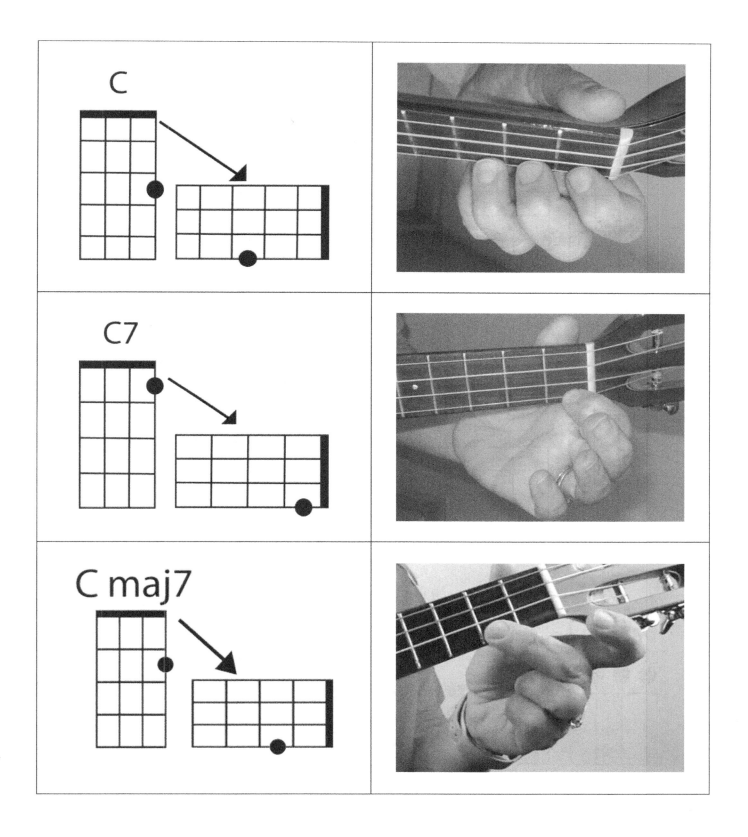

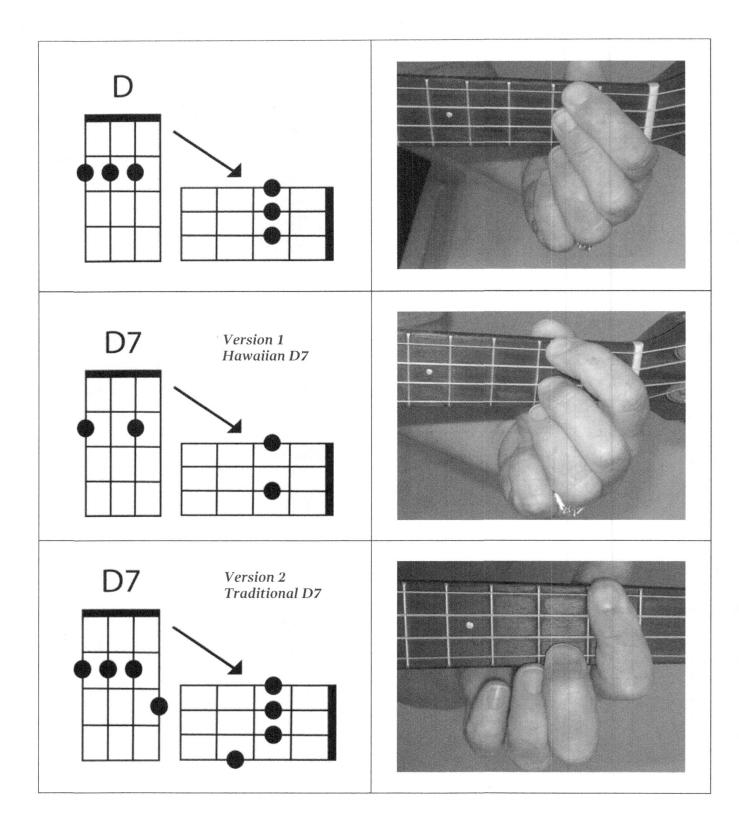

D

D7   *Version 1*
Hawaiian D7

D7   *Version 2*
Traditional D7

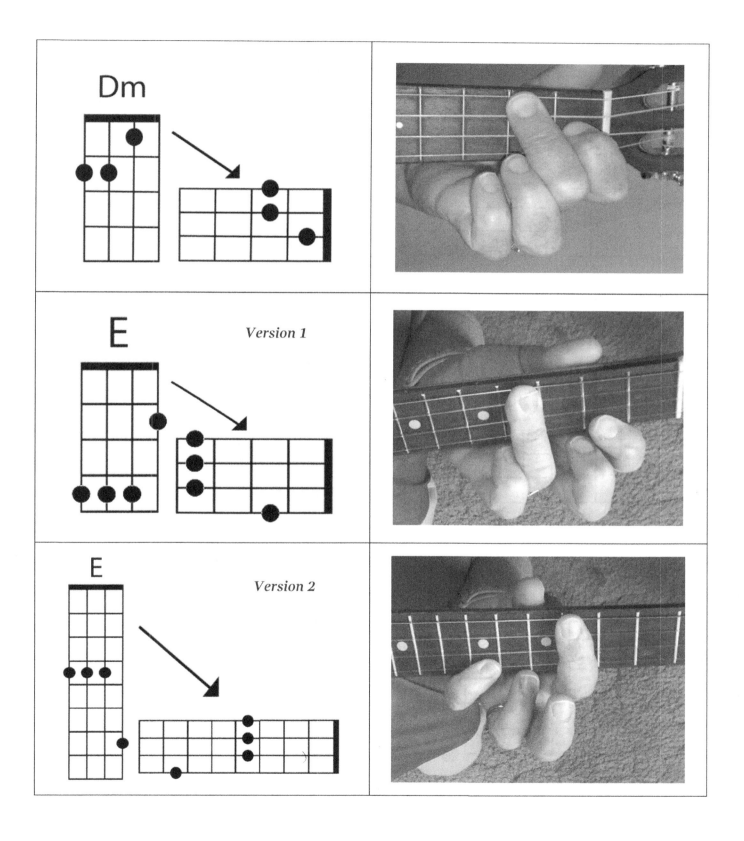

Dm

E — *Version 1*

E — *Version 2*

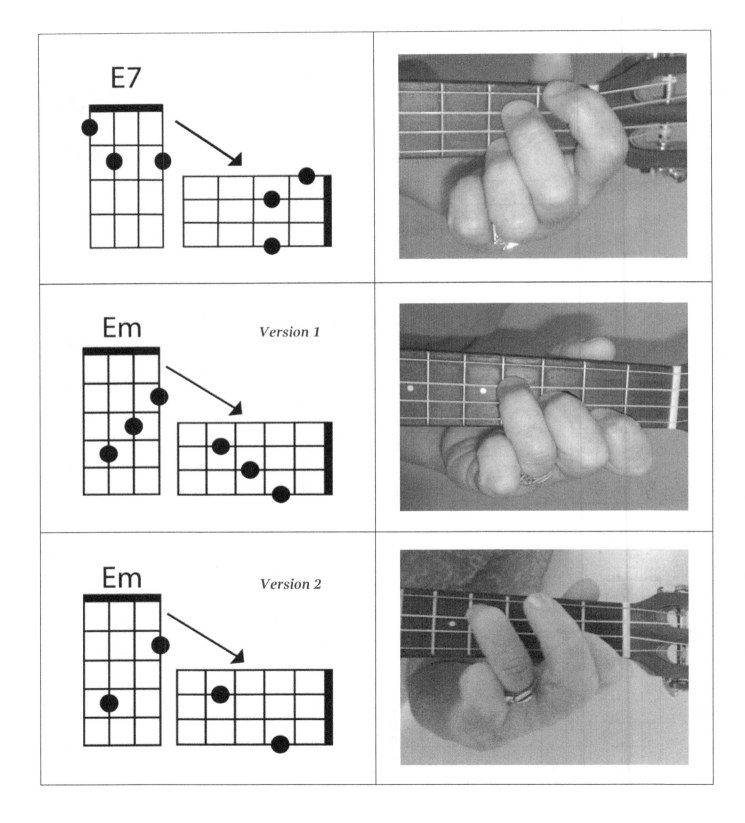

E7

Em   *Version 1*

Em   *Version 2*

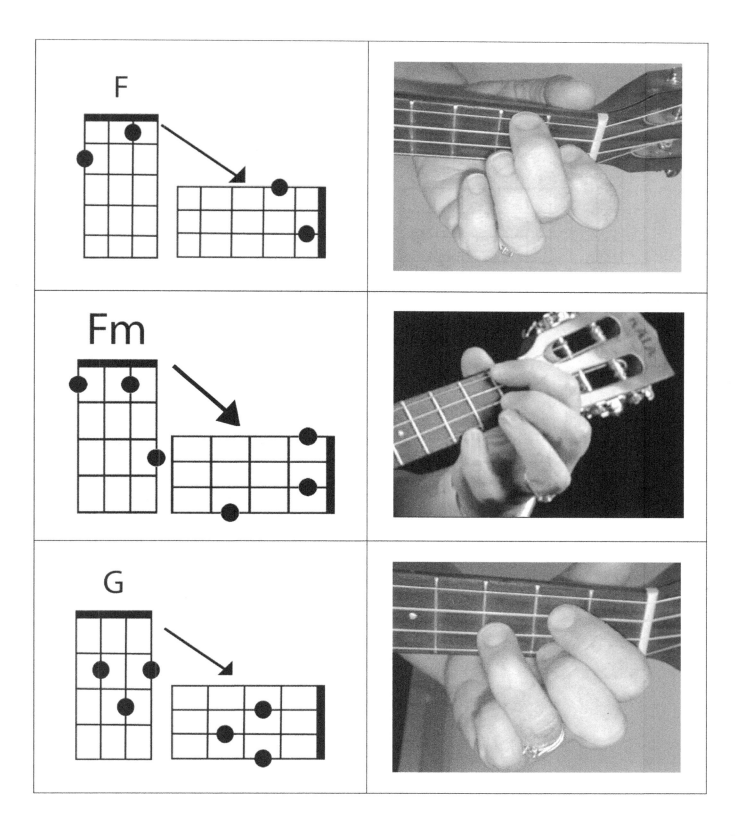

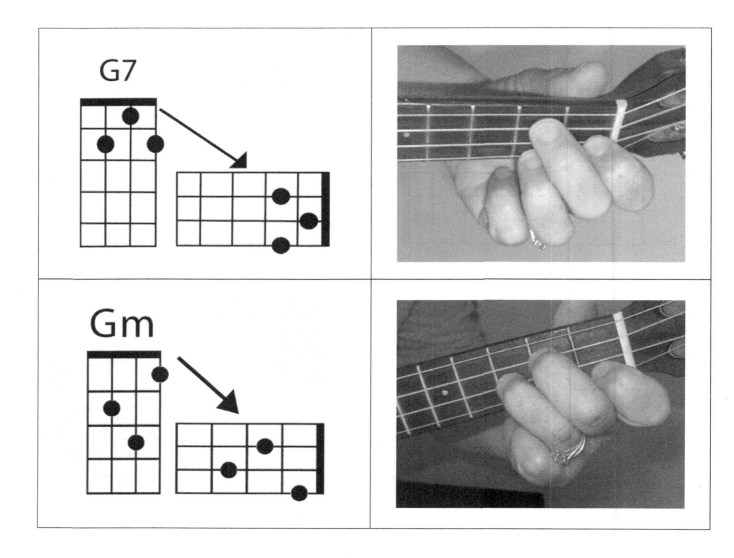

About the Ukulele Sisters

Jenny Peters is a Grammy nominated full time music educator in the Chicago area. She has taught thousands of beginners on a variety of instruments during her many years of teaching.

Jenny developed her unique beginner-friendly method of teaching ukulele when she learned to play in order to include ukulele to her fourth grade General Music classes. She has gone on to become a popular YouTube ukulele personality who owns seven different kinds of ukuleles!

Jenny and Rebecca have now written six books in the Beginning Ukulele Songs series: Book 1, *21 Songs in 6 Days Learn Ukulele the Easy Way*; Book 2, *Easy Ukulele Songs: Five with Five Chords*; Book 3, *21 Easy Ukulele Songs for Christmas*; Book 4, *21 MORE Songs in 6 Days: Learn Intermediate Ukulele the Easy Way*; Book 5, *21 Easy Ukulele Folk Songs*, and Book 6, *21 Easy Ukulele Hymns*.

The Illinois Music Educators Association has invited Jenny to do presentations on how to teach ukulele, and she has written articles on the subject for the magazine of the Illinois chapter of the American String Teachers Association. She is a member of the National Association for Music Education (NaFME), the American String Teachers Association (ASTA) and the American Society of Composers, Authors and Publishers (ASCAP). Jenny plays six other instruments besides ukulele: piano, violin, viola, cello, bass and organ. She currently heads a successful elementary and middle school orchestra program. Before that she taught Elementary General Music for ten years.

Jenny has served on the faculties of Lake Forest College and the College of Lake County. She taught piano, violin and chamber music at the Music Institute of Chicago and the Lake Forest Music Institute. She holds a Master of Music in Piano Performance from the University of Illinois and Bachelor of Music in Piano Performance from the University of Washington. She earned her teacher's certification from Trinity International University to share her passion for music with students of diverse backgrounds.

Rebecca Bogart has been introducing beginners of all ages to music for over 40 years. She believes that helping more people play music makes the world a better place.

She learned to play ukulele from her sister Jenny using the method taught in the Beginning Ukulele Songs series. While she has spent countless hours playing music with two hands at the piano, learning to have the left-hand fret chords while the right hand strummed was a surprisingly challenging experience! Rebecca brings a ukulele beginner's perspective to the Ukulele Sisters' writing team.

Rebecca has been passionate about the piano and music her entire life. She has played for audiences in Italy, taught master classes at Harvard and won more than a few piano competitions. She made her solo debut at Carnegie Hall in early 2014. Several of Rebecca's piano students have won national and international awards and appeared on NPR's radio show "From the Top." She has been a featured presenter at the California Music Teachers Association and has recorded a CD of American solo piano music *American Retrospective*. She completed her Masters degree in Piano at the San Francisco Conservatory of Music.

Jenny Peters jenny@ukulele.io

Rebecca Bogart rebecca@ukulele.io

facebook.com/UkuleleSisters/

youtube.com/c/Ukuleleio

instagram.com/jennypeters.theukulelesisters

Made in the USA
Las Vegas, NV
27 December 2024